T0182416

THIS EDITION
Editorial Management by Oriel Square
Produced for DK by WonderLab Group LLC
Jennifer Emmett, Erica Green, Kate Hale, *Founders*

Editor Maya Myers; **Photography Editor** Nicole DiMella; **Managing Editor** Rachel Houghton;
Designers Project Design Company; **Researcher** Michelle Harris;
Copy Editor Lori Merritt; **Indexer** Connie Binder; **Proofreader** Susan K. Hom;
Authenticity Reader Dr. Naomi R. Caldwell; **Series Reading Specialist** Dr. Jennifer Albro

First American Edition, 2024
Published in the United States by DK Publishing, a division of Penguin Random House LLC
1745 Broadway, 20th Floor, New York, NY 10019

A catalog record for this book is available from the Library of Congress.
HC ISBN: 978-0-7440-9450-3
PB ISBN: 978-0-7440-9449-7

DK books are available at special discounts when purchased in bulk for sales promotions, premiums, fund-raising,
or educational use. For details, contact:
DK Publishing Special Markets, 1745 Broadway, 20th Floor, New York, NY 10019
SpecialSales@dk.com

Printed and bound in China

The publisher would like to thank the following for their kind permission to reproduce their images:
a=above; c=center; b=below; l=left; r=right; t=top; b/g=background
Alamy Stock Photo: Ton Koene 1, 3, 4–5, 7b, 8tl, 8crb, 9t, 11t, 11b, 12b, 12–13, 14, 15, 16tr, 16–17, 18–19, 19cr, 20, 21,
22–23, 28, 30cla, 30cl, 30clb, 30bl; **Dreamstime.com:** Arkadiy Chumakov 17tr, Jim Cumming 27br, Flyingrussian
25ca, Mikelane45 10bl, Slowmotiongli 25tr, Steveheap 23tr, Iryna Volina 6tr; **Getty Images:** Grazyna Wilk-Scott /
500px 26–27t, 27br (Background), Brian Summers / Design Pics 8b, DigitalVision / Paul Souders 29, Moment Open
/ Vilhjalmur Ingi Vilhjalmsson 10crb; **Getty Images / iStock:** Michal_edo 18bc; **Acacia Johnson:** 24b, 30tl;
Shutterstock.com: Max Forgues 29cra, Paul Loewen 25tl

Cover images: *Front:* **Alamy Stock Photo:** Ton Koene; *Back:* **123RF.com:** hayatikayhan clb;
Dreamstime.com: Onyxprj cra

All other images © Dorling Kindersley Limited
For more information see: www.dkimages.com

www.dk.com

An Arctic Childhood

Jillian Metchooyeah and Maya Myers

Contents

Welcome to Gjoa Haven

Ullaakkut [OO-lah-coot]! It is still dark in Gjoa Haven [JO hay-ven], also called Uqsuqtuuq. Gjoa Haven is a hamlet in Nunavut, Canada. It is very far north. For about a month in the summer, it is light outside all the time.

Gjoa Haven

For about a month in the winter, it is dark outside all the time.
Now, it is spring. People wake up in the dark. It's time for Pauloosie to get ready for school.

Getting Ready

Pauloosie and his mother, Anaana [ah-NAA-na], eat oatmeal and dried fish. In Gjoa Haven, food arrives on a boat. Some food is flown in on an airplane. This makes the food very expensive.

It is cold outside.
Pauloosie wears layers
of clothes to stay warm.
He wears long pants and
a long-sleeved shirt. He
wears snow pants and a
warm parka.

View from the Bus

Here comes the bus! Snow crunches under the tires. Pauloosie looks out the window.
An Arctic fox leaves tracks in the snow.
A qimmiq [KIM-ick] watches the fox.

qimmiq

Arctic fox

Many houses are raised above the ground. This keeps their heat from melting the frozen earth. This way, the houses won't sink.

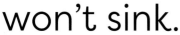

School Time

It's time for class. Pauloosie is learning Inuktitut. He practices speaking Inuktitut [in-OOK-tih-tut] words. He writes the words in his notebook.

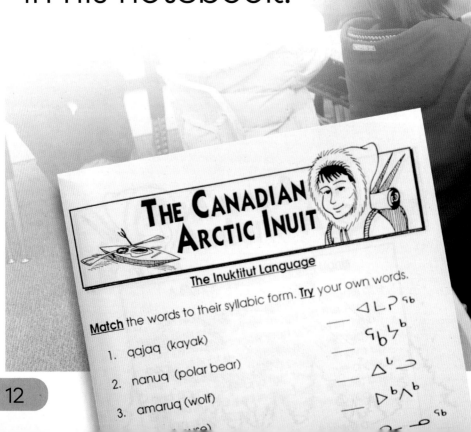

THE CANADIAN ARCTIC INUIT

The Inuktitut Language

Match the words to their syllabic form. Try your own words.

1. qajaq (kayak)
2. nanuq (polar bear)
3. amaruq (wolf)

ᐊᒪᕈᖅ
ᖅᔭᖅ
ᐊᓄᖅ
ᐅᖃᐱᖅ
ᖅ

Pauloosie gets lunch from the cafeteria. He sits with his friends. They share food with each other.

Recess time! Pauloosie
and his friends put on
their snow pants, parkas,
mitts, and hats. The sun
is bright, but it is still very
cold. Snow is everywhere!

They play hockey on the snow. Pauloosie practices his wrist shot.

A Quick Ride Home

Pauloosie's father, Ataata [ah-TAA-ta], picks him up after school. They ride on a snowmobile.

A willow ptarmigan [TAR-mih-gun] blends into the snow. The snowmobile scares the bird away! Ataata drops Pauloosie off at home. Anaana has his hockey gear ready. She will take him to the arena for practice.

Hockey Practice

In the dressing room, Pauloosie puts on his pads. He puts on his jersey. He ties up his ice skates. Finally, he buckles his helmet. He's ready to hit the ice!

He shows the team his wrist shot. He scores a goal!

Visiting

After practice, Pauloosie visits his grandparents. They are at their hunting camp. There is an iglu at the camp.

Pauloosie plays with Ataatattiaq [a-TAA-ta-tsi-ack] and the dogs. The dogs help them hunt.

Anaanattiaq [a-NAA-na-tsi-ack] is cooking meat from the hunt. She makes muktuk. Muktuk is made of whale skin and blubber.

Anaanattiaq cuts the meat with an ulu [oo-lu].

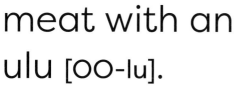

Community Feast

Pauloosie and his family bring muktuk to the community center. There is a community feast. Many people from the town are there.

Arctic char

caribou

muktuk

Pauloosie, his family, and their friends eat together. They eat some caribou, some fish, and some muktuk.
After they finish eating, families pack the extra food to take home.

Northern Lights

What a busy day. Now, it is time to go home. Pauloosie almost falls asleep in the car.

But wow! The northern lights are out! They light up the sky. An owl swoops by.

Hoo! Hoo!

Good Night!

At home, Pauloosie takes a bath. Splish, splash! He pretends he is a polar bear, swimming in the water.

Pauloosie puts on pajamas. He snuggles into bed. Ataata tells him a story about magical little people. Pauloosie yawns.

Good night, Ataata.
Good night, Anaana.
Good night, beautiful
lights.

Glossary

community
a group of people who live in a place and help care for one another

hamlet
small town

iglu
a shelter built from snow, used while hunting

parka
a warm coat with a hood often lined with real or fake fur

snowmobile
a vehicle used to travel over snow

Index

Quiz

Answer the questions to see what you have learned. Check your answers with an adult.

1. How does food get delivered to Gjoa Haven?

2. Why are houses in Gjoa Haven raised off the ground?

3. What tool does Pauloosie's grandmother use to prepare muktuk?

4. What does Pauloosie see on the ride home from the community feast?

5. What is Pauloosie's bedtime story about?

1. By plane or boat 2. To help prevent the frozen earth from melting 3. An ulu 4. The northern lights
5. Magical little people